The Corps of Discovery

Kristin Cashore

Contents

Rigby®

A Harcourt Achieve Imprint

www.Rigby.com
1-800-531-5015

The Unknown West

In the early 1800s, most of the American **population** was settled in the East, near the Atlantic Ocean. Few Americans had even seen what we call the American West. It was an unknown wilderness and a land where American Indians lived.

In the year 1804, a team of **explorers** set out on a journey that would change this. Together they blazed a trail across America, all the way to the Pacific Ocean. Three important members of this **expedition** were Meriwether Lewis, William Clark, and a Shoshone Indian woman named Sacagawea.

The United States in the Early 1800s

OREGON TERRITORY

MICHIGAN TERRITORY

VERMONT

MAINE

NEW HAMPSHIRE

MASSACHUSETTS

ILLINOIS TERRITORY

NEW YORK

CONNECTICUT

PENNSYLVANIA

LOUISIANA TERRITORY

INDIANA TERRITORY

OHIO

DELAWARE

VIRGINIA

NEW SPAIN

KENTUCKY

TENNESSEE

NORTH CAROLINA

SOUTH CAROLINA

MISSISSIPPI TERRITORY

GEORGIA

NEW ORLEANS TERRITORY

NEW SPAIN

Most Americans lived in the East, not knowing what the West was like.

Meriwether Lewis

Born in Virginia in 1774, Meriwether Lewis grew to love the wilderness. He became an excellent hunter and learned all he could about plants and animals. As a young man, he served in the Army. In 1801 he became the personal **secretary** to President Thomas Jefferson.

President Jefferson had wanted to explore the West for a very long time. He thought Meriwether Lewis might just be the man for the job. Jefferson asked Lewis to begin planning the journey.

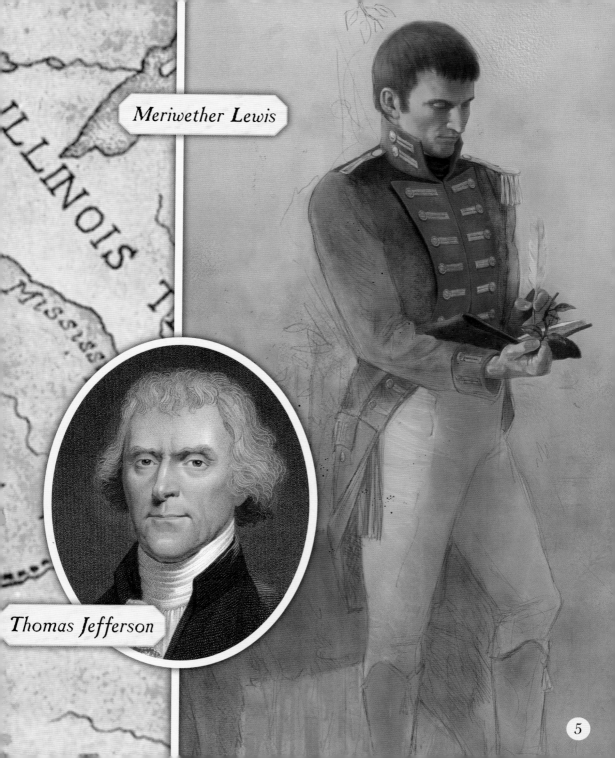

ILLINOIS T

MISSISS

Meriwether Lewis

Thomas Jefferson

Lewis took his new job to heart. He learned all he could about the people, land, and wildlife of the American West. He studied the science of plants and animals. And he learned how to use the stars to tell his location and his direction. He also made long lists of the supplies he would need for the journey.

Items Needed for Expedition

Compass
Telescope
Plotting Instruments
Cloth for Tents
Iron Corn Mill
Mosquito Curtains
Fishing Hooks
Fishing Lines
Soap
Writing Paper
Ink
Crayons
Flannel Shirts
Shoes
Coats
Woolen Pants

Lewis made long lists of items needed for the expedition.

Lewis did not let President Jefferson down. He teamed up with other explorers and journeyed to the West. During the expedition, he was strong and brave, and he never gave up even during great struggles. After the expedition, Lewis was given rewards of land and money. He was also named the **governor** of the Louisiana Territory.

After all these honors, his life after the journey was sadly cut short. Lewis died in 1809 at the age of 35. He is buried in Tennessee.

Many people today visit his gravesite in Tennessee.

William Clark

William Clark was born in Virginia in 1770. His older brother, George Rogers Clark, was a general in the Revolutionary War. Clark learned all about surviving in the wilderness from his brother George.

When Clark grew older he served in the Army. He learned to build forts, draw maps, and travel through dangerous lands. At one point, a young man named Meriwether Lewis served under his command. Clark and Lewis got along well, and they became good friends.

William Clark

Years later, when Lewis realized that his expedition to the West needed more than one captain, he thought of William Clark. Lewis wrote to Clark asking him to join the expedition, and Clark wrote a letter back in which he agreed.

July, 1803

To Meriwether Lewis:
My friend, I assure you no man lives with whom I would prefer to undertake such a trip as yourself.

William Clark

William Clark's map making skills were important to the expedition.

William Clark was daring, strong, and smart. On the expedition to the West, he and Lewis made a wonderful team. When the explorers returned home, Clark was also given land, money, and jobs as a reward. He was in charge of American Indian concerns in the West and tried very hard to sway the government into treating American Indians fairly. He also became the governor of the Missouri Territory.

Clark named his first son Meriwether Lewis Clark in honor of his friend. Clark died in 1838.

Sacagawea

Sacagawea was born sometime in the late 1780s in what is now known as Idaho. Sacagawea was a member of the Shoshone Indian tribe who lived in the Rocky Mountains. When she was about 12 years old, she was kidnapped by Hidatsa Indians. Her kidnappers brought her to their home in what is now known as North Dakota.

It was not strange in this place and time for American Indian women to be bought and sold as slaves. Sacagawea was sold to a fur trader named Toussaint Charbonneau who then married her.

Lewis, Clark, and their team of explorers headed for the West and spent the winter of 1804 near Sacagawea's village. Sacagawea gave birth to a son, Jean-Baptiste, in Lewis and Clark's fort.

Sacagawea

Lewis and Clark's Fort

As Lewis and Clark learned more about Sacagawea, they understood that she spoke Shoshone. This was important information for Lewis and Clark as they headed farther west. Lewis and Clark asked Sacagawea to join them as a **translator**. If they needed more supplies, she would be able to work out a trade with American Indians who spoke Shoshone. Sacagawea and her husband agreed to go on the journey with the explorers. The baby traveled with them on Sacagawea's back.

After the expedition, Sacagawea's husband was given land and money as a reward, but Sacagawea was given nothing. It is believed that Sacagawea died in 1812 at a very young age.

Sacagawea carried her son on her back as seen in the picture above.

American Indian Groups in the West

Chinook

Wishram

Blackfeet

Assiniboin

Hidatsa

Nez Perce

Clatsop

Walla Walla

Shoshone

Mandan

Tillamook

Arikara

Teton Sioux

Yankton Sioux

Oto

Missouri

N

W

E

S

The Corps of Discovery

You have learned about the separate lives of Lewis, Clark, and Sacagawea. But what happened when they came together to explore the American West?

It was certainly not an easy journey. It began in May of 1804 near St. Louis, Missouri. The group of explorers, who would later be called the **Corps** of Discovery, started up the Missouri River in three boats. By November they had reached what is now North Dakota, where Lewis and Clark met Sacagawea for the first time. The Corps of Discovery spent the winter in a fort near her village.

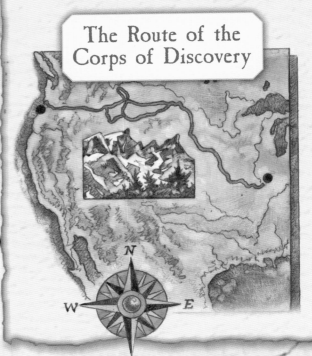

The Route of the Corps of Discovery

When spring came, a group numbering 33 people, including Sacagawea and her baby, set out west on the Missouri River. In what is now Montana, they ran into the Great Falls of the Missouri. It took the explorers nearly a month to carry the boats and the supplies around these waterfalls!

The Purpose of the Corps of Discovery

What did President Jefferson want the Corps of Discovery to do?

- To learn about the plants and animals of the West
- To map the West and find the best routes for trading
- To make friends with the American Indians in the West
- To tell any people they met in the West that this land now belonged to the United States

Lewis and Clark with Mandan Indians

As the group pushed its way west, Sacagawea began to recognize **landmarks** from her childhood. When the Corps reached the land of the Shoshone people, Sacagawea discovered that the chief was her long-lost brother! As Lewis and Clark had hoped, Sacagawea was able to help them buy the horses they needed to cross the Rocky Mountains.

A Time Line of the Corps of Discovery

October 1804 In North Dakota, the Corps builds a winter fort across the river from Sacagawea's village.

April 1805 The Corps heads west on the Missouri River.

1804		1805					
May	October	January	February	March	April	May	June

May 1804 The Corps of Discovery begins traveling up the Missouri River near St. Louis, Missouri.

February 1805 Sacagawea gives birth to her son in Lewis and Clark's fort.

June 1805 The Corps takes almost a month to travel around the Great Falls of the Missouri River.

The Rocky Mountains were steep and wild. The Corps almost starved during the crossing! The Corps then traveled west on the Clearwater River, the Snake River, and the Columbia River into the states known today as Oregon and Washington.

In November 1805, Lewis, Clark, Sacagawea, and their Corps of Discovery set eyes on the Pacific Ocean for the first time.

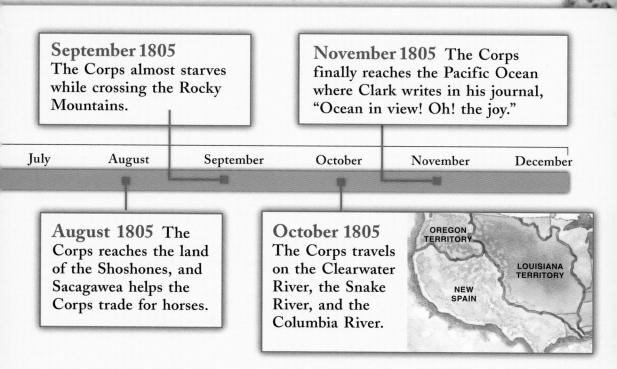

September 1805
The Corps almost starves while crossing the Rocky Mountains.

November 1805 The Corps finally reaches the Pacific Ocean where Clark writes in his journal, "Ocean in view! Oh! the joy."

July   August   September   October   November   December

August 1805 The Corps reaches the land of the Shoshones, and Sacagawea helps the Corps trade for horses.

October 1805 The Corps travels on the Clearwater River, the Snake River, and the Columbia River.

OREGON TERRITORY

LOUISIANA TERRITORY

NEW SPAIN

The expedition would not have succeeded without Lewis, Clark, or Sacagawea. Lewis kept journals about the trip. He wrote in great detail about the animals and the plants he saw. He collected samples of wildlife for later study, and he remained brave and strong even when the going got tough.

Clark was the mapmaker and artist of the expedition. He made drawings of landscapes and animals. He was good at communicating with American Indians, and he was also good at coming up with solutions to problems the Corps faced.

William Clark's drawings showed the kinds of animals they saw on their journey.

Sacagawea was very helpful to Lewis and Clark. She helped the Corps find their way through Shoshone lands. She collected plants, roots, and berries that were used as food and medicine. When a boat tipped over, Sacagawea rescued the journals, medicines, and other items that washed overboard. And throughout the journey, Sacagawea helped Lewis and Clark make peace with the people they met. The presence of a woman and a baby in the Corps helped many American Indians see Lewis and Clark as friendly people.

The Corps of Discovery was considered to be a great success. Even though there were accidents, sicknesses, dangerous waters, grizzly bears, rattlesnakes, cold temperatures, and near starvation, only one group member died. And Lewis and Clark returned to the East with a huge amount of information about the American wilderness.

Lewis, Clark, and Sacagawea opened the doors to the American West, and, in time, the country grew to be 50 states strong!

American Indians After Lewis and Clark

Lewis and Clark made friends with many American Indians in the West, but not everyone was respectful of American Indians. When people began to move west, American Indians were pushed aside and many of them were killed. Lewis and Clark might have been sad to know that their expedition marked the beginning of a very hard time for American Indians in the West.

The United States Today

WASHINGTON
MONTANA
NORTH DAKOTA
MINNESOTA
VERMONT MAINE
NEW HAMPSHIRE
OREGON
IDAHO
SOUTH DAKOTA
WISCONSIN
MASSACHUSETTS
NEW YORK
RHODE ISLAND
WYOMING
MICHIGAN
PENNSYLVANIA
CONNECTICUT
NEW JERSEY
NEBRASKA
IOWA
OHIO
NEVADA
UTAH
COLORADO
KANSAS
MISSOURI
INDIANA
ILLINOIS
WEST VIRGINIA
DELAWARE
MARYLAND
VIRGINIA
CALIFORNIA
KENTUCKY
ARIZONA
NEW MEXICO
OKLAHOMA
ARKANSAS
TENNESSEE
NORTH CAROLINA
SOUTH CAROLINA
PACIFIC OCEAN
GEORGIA
ATLANTIC OCEAN
TEXAS
ALABAMA
LOUISIANA
MISSISSIPPI
FLORIDA
ALASKA
HAWAII

*After **Lewis, Clark,** and **Sacagawea** explored the **West,** America grew to become a nation of 50 states.*

Glossary

corps a group of people working together for the same purpose

expedition a journey to new lands

explorers travelers who go to new lands in order to learn

governor an elected official who is head of a state

landmarks objects that mark the land and help people to know where they are

population the number of people in an area

secretary an official in charge of a department in government

translator someone who changes words into a different language